just like that

just like that

Poems, Paintings, and Practices

g i s e l a   s t r o m e y e r

Epigraph Books
Rhinebeck, New York

Just Like That: Poems, Paintings, and Practices
© 2019 by Gisela Stromeyer

ISBN 978-1-948796-60-6

Library of Congress Control Number 2019936951

Book design by Colin Rolfe

Photo on page 149 by Joseph Jastrab
Photo on page 152 by Wallie Wolfgruber
Photos on pages 30 and 149 originally taken by Joseph Jastrab,
painted over by Gisela Stromeyer
Photo on page 152 by Wallie Wolfgruber

Epigraph Books
22 East Market Street, Suite 304
Rhinebeck, New York 12572
(845) 876-4861
epigraphps.com

Contents

Foreword   IX

Introduction.   XIII

The food I need.   3

Union with Source   4

Just Like That   5

Mistakes   6

Body wisdom   8

Who is crazy, you or I?   9

Who are You Anyway?   10

Promise   11

Loss   13

Who are You?   14

Sometimes   15

Weave   16

Trust   18

Decide   19

What Does it Mean to Wake Up?   20

Creation   21

Divine Plan   23

Robot   24

Choice   25

Trust   26

Impermanence   27

Water is Alive.   28

This will burn you for sure.   31

This morning   32

Sacred Water   33

Being   34

Water   35

Request   37

Resilience   39

Currents   40

New   41

Heart,   42

And even so,   43

Women   45

Receiving   47

Now   48

Embodiment   49

Mystery   51

The Big Questions   52

Tender   53

The Wisdom of Not Knowing   54

Try that!   56

When Life Becomes Small   57

Self Love   59

Sehnsucht   61

Realness   62

Loss   63

Pond   65

Vulnerable   66

No Worries!   67

Let's just let it all go,   68

To Let Go and Listen   69

Take Care of Yourself   70

Empty   71

Balance   72

The Power of the Void   74

Love   75

Cruelty   77

Content   78

Remember   79

Is that you on the cross?   81

Intimacy   83

In-between   85

Fear is part of change   87

Relax   88

Honest   89

Void Creation   90

Presence   91

Sun   92

Flying Fire   93

Spirals   95

Beauty   96

Stop!   97

Too Much   98

Why? 100
Really important 101
What is 102
Truth 104
Beauty Within 105
How do I live the life I am "meant" to live? 106
Same Old 107
Small 109
Empathy 110
Holy 111
Vibration 112
Everything 113
Potential 115
Purpose 116
Learn 117
Drink 118
Pain 120
To Not Know 121
The deep longing that makes you love more 122
Do you want to play in the mud? 123
Loslassen 124
Depression 126
Clinging 127
The spiritual Can-Opener 128
Beauty 129
Moment 130
Protection 131
Relations 132
Love 133
Destiny 134
Teacher 135
Serpent 137
Mistakes are Ideas of the Mind 138
Becoming 139
Wake Up ! 140
Closed Door 141
Love Making 142
Creative Force 144
Such longing in us for that holy place 145
To Be Close 146

Shift   147
Good and Bad   148
The Seed of the Void   150
To Become Real   151
The Right Soil—The Right Moment   153
So Unbearably Vulnerable   154

Practices: 155
Void Meditation   156
Black mirror practice   157
Practice to help with pain and emotional upset   159
Practice to merge with your surrounding   161
Practice to be able to shift perspective   164
Titration between dark and light   166
Walking meditation   169
Woman Meditations:
first exploration   171
second exploration   173
third exploration   174
fourth exploration   175
Lower mouth meditation   176
Mirror meditation to increase self love   178

Acknowledgments   181
About the Author   182

Foreword

We all had moments when we get up in the morning, looking out the window, inhale deeply and sigh. We just went through a challenge, a powerful life-changing event that shook us. We look in the mirror and wonder, what is this life about? Where is this journey taking me? What am I doing? Why bother? The answer to these questions and many others lies in this book of poems:

"Just Like That." Gisela Stromeyer takes us on a journey through life, with the nonjudgmental observational purity of a child, one that doesn't miss a thing; the fearlessness of warrioress, who faces the wind; the wizard who sees magic in everything; the priestess who elevates each mundane chore into a spiritual ecstasy, a lover who bewitches us to delve into self -love, and back to the child who embraces our journey with wonder and without questioning.

A full circle of the human voyage elevated, celebrated, rejoiced and embraced. Each moment a new, from observing water, its fluidity, honoring its form and substance and offering gratitude, to getting up and see the world as an endowmeant, and finding love inside to offer gratitude, be thankful for the presence of life itself.

With poems such as:

Impermanence

Today I am looking out of the window
I see the shadow that a tree casts in the sun.
I love the pattern,
a weaving of light and darkness...
Some things are always there,
like the shadow of a tree
when the sun is out and

some things always change in a movement.
The wisdom is
to know what is what
and to go with the flow of the movement,
appreciating what is.

Or this one:

This morning

This morning,
I tell you, is special!
Like every morning, I would say.
Let us make an effort to wake up,
to breathe our hearts out into the world,
our bodies,
our life.
For we need more love inside
and out to balance all that is happening
in our world.

I know Gisela Stromeyer, I feel like I have known her for many life times. I am privileged and grateful to have met a person who holds such a range of talents, abilities, and capacity to embrace, to create, to birth, to hold and to turn the mundane into Magic.

I sought Gisela years back on an advice of a friend. I was hurt, I was in pain, and I was looking to heal. I did heal largely thanks to her guidance, support and love, and to my bewilderment I discovered that there are people like her in the world, who elevates everything they touch, and anyone who cross their path.

I became aware over the years of her poetry, her writing, experienced her workshops, healing power, and her teachings. Each time I read or heard her, I felt empowered, more joyful, as if I just drank a magical potion, a healing substance, a remedy for the soul, a balm for the heart, words that lift the edges of my lips and forced the inner smile out .My encounter with her changed my life.

Everyone who meets her inevitably changes, gets elevated, healed, transformed, and gifted. Her presence is radiant; her laugh contagious, her heart is large, compassion unlimited which encompasses the pains of those around her. She knows pain intimately, she understands loss, and she experienced hurt. Gisela took the challenges life offered her and transmuted them into a legacy, not just for herself but for the benefit of all who comes in contact with her.

Gisela Stromeyer, is a renaissance women, a rare combination of tenacity, softness, brilliance, compassion, honesty, clarity, fragility, vulnerability, outer strength combined with inner power. My life was enriched, expanded, healed and so do the life of many souls who crossed her path.

Gisela is a light that shines where ever she goes, and this book is a way for her light to travel without her physically needing to be present, a gift for me that I intend to share with my loved ones. For some time now, I felt that we should all benefit from her wisdom, her melody, her beauty and here it is. I am eternally grateful to have met such a beautiful human being and I am thankful to have had the honor to write the forward to her book of poetry Just Like That."

Life is becoming exceedingly faster, more intense. We are asked to deal with so many more challenges than ever before, and none are simple. Life is complex spectrum of shades from the lightest to the darkest. Often, we get lost in the maze, where to go what to choose, how to best walk the path of truth of light and remain with our heart wide open and receptive. Gisela's poems guide us back to the basics; she highlights the notions of beauty, which emanate from each experience, from each breath, her words act like a fulcrum, scaffolding, allowing us to remain centered. This book of poems, meditations, exercises, allow us to rest in the spaces between the words, a reprieve from the chase, she encourages us to slow down to look at everything with fresh eyes, to inhale and exhale with a new perspective, to self-inject love where it lacks, to Om, and call for peace when we are lost, to find the home we all yearn for in our own hearts, to accept and love ourselves truly.

With eternal Gratitude and love.
Dror Ashuah

Introduction.

I wish for this book to be like a seed drifting into the world to find its
place,
its fertile ground.
It may be useful to someone that needs just a small message
in a moment of doubt,
a thread of gold to know which way to face,

That would mean a lot to me.

I am hoping the perspectives that my life has to offer will open
some doors for another

I wish to send this seed of my deep connection to life
and my process of opening my perception and my energy, into the
world.
Hopefully a bee will land and take some pollen with her, book
pollen,
wisdom pollen, and so it might just make its way to you,
since you are reading this.

Writing these messages and poems is a very healing process for
me.
It is a beautiful feeling to find a form of expression for what I feel
and know to be true. And once in words,
it can carry the sound into the word.
The message becomes much easier to share.

Just open any page and perhaps that is the message for you in this
moment.

magic is important to me—
magic, that happens in small ways.
The deep touching of our human hearts.
The moment of deep understanding and love.
The moment of truth that leaves us naked.
The moment, when we all feel the presence of magic.
The moment we can feel the strings that connect us all.
That is the blessing.

My process of opening my senses,
my energy,
my consciousness,
is reflected in my words—
and so is my gift to give.

May it serve well.

The food I need.

Please, please be yourself !
So I can love you !
Don't try on other skins
to ensure love,
thinking this, thinking that,
about yourself.

If you are not you,
there is no place for my love.
It will never be able to enter.
And so,
how can we love each other?

And then again,
I remember that love just is,
and does not need
a place.

Union with Source

If you would ask me, "why are you here?"
I would say, "to serve you."
And if you would ask me "how do I serve you?'
I would say, "by dying into you."

For you,
I bow my head in awe and gratitude,
a head that can be
haughty with arrogance and pride.

For you,
I will be quiet and listen to the deep sounds of being.

For you,
I let my heart open, a longing heart for deep connection,
a heart that sometimes wants to claw and grab in great
desperation
like a hurt child.

For you,
I open my womb, my lips ...my ocean,
a womb and lips that long for deep ecstatic union.

And so the wind caresses the hair on my bare skin,
calling forth love,
and I stand in front of you naked,
in flesh and blood,
swimming in a sea of longing

wet and new.

Just Like That

It feels to me
it's time to claim your place,
your love,
your space.

Do you feel it?

There is a fire burning inside
that makes it possible to claim,
to have,
to be.

And nobody can
stop you.

Just like that

Mistakes

The problem is not so much making a mistake
or hurting someone,
it happens.

The problem is
when you don't correct
what has felt wrong in your heart
with the
other.
There is an opening of becoming closer,
in this process of being honest
to yourself and
another...
maybe that is the process of
growing together,
and the purpose of the mistake.

Body wisdom

Know your body.
The keys of knowledge
are there to be explored.
The wisdom is all hidden within.

First, we find the keys
And once we open
the doors of our energy,
we discover,
that we are so much more then our body,
and that love
is the fluid
that opens it
all.

Who is crazy, you or I?

"Crazy is good,"
shouts a voice
from deep inside my being.
It did not seem so
When I was a young child
feeling strange for
the things I loved.

But ... really, "crazy is good!"
shouts the voice again, even louder,
insisting.

Crazy is good?

And once I am back again,
after having ventured out into the world.

Call it crazy, call it wise,
it is what I love
and it is leading
me well.

Who are You Anyway?

A woman friend said to me,
"god wants me to do that,
and he said this to me..."

I wondered where her god was,
who is he ?
Far away with a male voice
she is a female.
Who is talking to her ?

I am thinking to myself,
the voice I hear is an inner voice, my voice.
My wisdom is guiding me.
The divine energy takes on my shape, my voice,
I am that !
I am here on this earth in this shape.
Why would it not take her shape?

The divine flows though all,
It is in all things, all people.
We are that!
It makes us responsible for our life!

If we really believe it,
feel it, are it,
well then we are one with existence
all worthlessness, all doubt,
all insecurity falls off us

because we are perfect as
the Devine

P r o m i s e

When you wake up in the morning
make a promise to yourself
that you will be a little
kinder today,
to yourself,
to others,
to the sky,
the air,
the water,
even the fire,
the animals and plants,
the life force in all things
and see
at the end of the day
what you have accomplished
and how you feel
about the day.

L o s s

When something breaks
that you love,
inside or outside,
object or relationship,
just know
the energy the object held
or the relationship contained
is now set
free.
It's not lost,
it is only without shape
for a moment.
You can have it again

if you wish.

Where are You?

if you feel your life is boring
and full of repetition
you feel unhappy about yourself,
then you are not in the moment.

When we are in the moment
we don't feel that way,
we don't think.
Only when we are outside
We judge
And make ourselves
unhappy.

Sometimes

When you find yourself
anxious, nervous, not wanting
to sit still...
It's time to take a breath.
Know there is something inside
that wants to be felt,
something angry,
something sad,
something
that you don't like feeling.
Turn towards it
feel!
meet it with your heart,
allow the content
to flow through you.

then you are back in the flow!

Weave

When I am sitting in the dark,
dark enough with just a little bit of light,
I am fortunate to find myself in a deep place,
my open heart still
I can see the pattern of life
swirling around me.
Fast and ever moving
in all directions
connecting us,

expressing all,

lines of colorful light,
shapes appearing and disappearing,
profoundly weaving me into their space
If I have courage, I stay awake and become one.
If I get afraid of knowing, it goes away.
Still I always feel blessed knowing it's there,
always there, the weave
that weaves us
all together.

Trust

When somebody in your life wronged you,
you feel the pain in your heart,
you wonder how to ever trust again?

Remember

you are infinite,
you have the power to transform something ugly
into something amazing.
This is how "bad" experiences serve us.
We are forced to find within us a way to handle them.
The part of us that can handle it, comes forward in this process
standing face-to-face with the pain and fear,
so that you know
that you have an amazing way to deal with life that liberates you.
And often in these bleak moments
there is a special friend that comes and helps,
unexpected,
because we need the help
and
pain made
an opening.

Decide

When I do not know how to decide,
when I have a hard time knowing,
but I need to make a choice,
I close my eyes,
I look from the inside,
at the landscape of the question
through the blackness of the void
to see where there is most light.
Once I see it,
I choose that,
whatever it is,
and trust.

What Does it Mean to Wake Up?

Everybody in the spiritual world tells me,
"Wake up"
the time is now!"
And I agree, and then what?
I wake up in the morning
and need a cup of coffee.
That works for that!
But to really wake up
out of the dream of my life takes different measures.
It takes consciousness,
it takes stopping and breathing consciously
to feel who I am,
to make space for the timid voice inside
to be heard
that voice knows how
to choose my next step well,
or just be with what is.
It takes courage
to make a different choice than everybody else
It takes courage
to face something inside
that make me feel afraid,
and to guide myself into an unknown territory
with a sense of

okayness.

It's a constant adventure!
If you lack this adventure
you might want to allow some change.
In that space between your habitual life patterns
and the new unfolding, is all the adventure you need.
Be prepared to be uncomfortable but more alive, more awake
than ever

Creation

Our creations unfold all the time.
It is just not always to our liking
and often we are not aware
we are doing the creating.
Our own creating
stays hidden from us.
We put it outside
and pretend it is happening to us.
But the act of creating
always happens inside.
It is our responsibility
to participate
with consciousness.

Divine Plan

We are all part of a divine plan
very unique to each of us
bringing forth our true being
in a complete way.
This "plan" links us together
in a powerful geometry of hearts
around the planet.
Each unique heart
brings forth its own power
and beauty

Each person is embodying the 'I am" in their unique way.
We all carry different aspects of the divine.
We are all equally important
and essential in this unfolding of heart energy.
We are doing our best to let this greater heart energy unfold
through us.
It is like the flower of life,
no center,
equal circles forming an endless web of connection ...
to serve oneness,
to serve love,
to raise vibration...
Even as I am writing this to you,
my heart is one of many...
We do our best to form one being!
nobody stays separate,
we do not have a leader,
no hierarchy,
only the unfolding of each brilliant,
beautiful heart in equal importance.
I am grateful to the light,
the divine source in all things,
that is guiding us,
all together and individually.

R o b o t

We all have a robot inside
that takes over
because
it thinks it can do the job best.
Don't let it!
Use your breath,
imagination,
and will
to stay

awake.

Choice

Since all ideas, teachings,
thinkings,
feelings
are just perspectives of what reality is.
And since there is no absolute truth,
you might as well choose something
you like,
something that suits you,
is you—
not one that you think might keep you safe
or sounds good.
All perspectives on the same subject
are like a bunch of flashlights shining on something in the dark,
that we are trying
to better see
and understand.
Each perspective is valuable
because each offers a little more
of what we are
exploring,
of what
Reality
is.

Trust

Trust in the flow of your own life.
We are all part of a larger divine flow
that is full of
creative potential.
Whatever we need can always reach us
leave the door open
and stay present and relaxed.

Impermanence

Today I am looking out of the window
I see the shadow that a tree casts in the sun.
I love the pattern,
a weaving of light and darkness...
Some things are always there,
like the shadow of a tree
when the sun is out and
some things always change in a movement.
The wisdom is
to know what is what
and to go with the flow of the movement,
appreciating what is.

Water is Alive.

It is a living being that is unbelievably sensitive
and moves through all creation.   It is not picky, it
reflects everything.
It resonates with all that   is on this planet and
beyond,
It's inner and outer movements   reflect change and absorb
what it comes in contact with.
It can shape and flow and change shape again and again,
continuously
bringing forth messages.

Water is moving through everything,
all the time, all over the planet, and
for such a long time has recorded all that has occurred.
It is connected to all.
It is one being.

Wherever you speak to water,
you speak with all of it,
on the whole planet and beyond.

Water has such a strong pull to become One

This must be true for me too and you
We are built of water,
we belong to water
we must know everything
and have a strong pull
to become one!

This will burn you for sure.

What is the passionate heart, the erotic longing
I am asking for?

The sensuous love,
this love, that is so powerful and potent that it takes the mind
away at once.

Filled with uncomfortable desire, full of vibrant energy, beaming
like the sun itself ...let us not get lost by lusty desire but be awed
by the sacred force that includes the deepest love.
The sacred flow of everything together as one ecstatic experience.

This will make you burn for sure.

Heat rising, sweat on my forehead, and eaten by desire to let go
and give into the wildest moment of all.

The fire of deep longing and fierce desire for sacred union is
burning
until there is nothing left
but wet birthing darkness.

This morning

This morning,
I tell you, is special!
Like every morning, I would say.
Let us make an effort to wake up,
to breathe our hearts out into the world,
our bodies,
our life.
For we need more love inside
and out to balance all that is happening
in our world.

Sacred Water

Water is one of the most healing substances,
life forms.
It is wise to honor it,
care for it,
making it sacred
again
then
you will be sacred.

Being

there is something
very powerful
about closing your eyes
sitting in darkness,
whenever you need
that space
of just being.

Water

When you discover
something is more alive or more conscious
than you expected
it is beautiful,
and also a little scary.
All of a sudden
there is more of a relationship then expected.

It is us
that is awakening
to an aliveness
that was sleeping
within us.

Request

...there is a request
in the air
that we grow
beyond our imagined boundaries
and include all,
that is waiting,
in our love and care,
it is a matter of allowing,
being,
no effort
necessary.

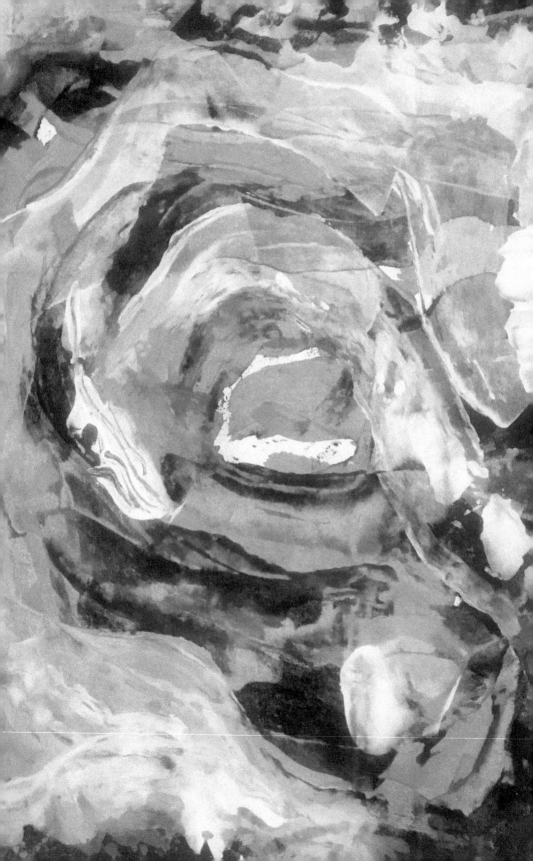

Resilience

Being...
at any moment
we have the possibility to rest,
to sit with ourselves and feel inside...
breathe
and just be.
Be,
and in the being,
empty,
and in the empty,
reset our being.

close your eyes
be at home in the darkness of this moment.
feel the comfort of the velvet blackness around you,
and then
a nagging thoughts say:
"listen to me, I am very important, you might forget this or that,
so you better jump into action, now
before its too late..."

Really ?

You might think to yourself.
And if you start laughing the thoughts slips away.
Thank god!
You just saved yourself.
In the quiet darkness,
all the outer demands are melting away,
The darkness deeply nourishes
And how could that not make you happy,
happy to be yourself,
happy to be with yourself.

Currents

There are currents of emotions,
there are currents of thought,
of ideas,
coming through all the time.
From everywhere and everybody.
We think we invented it,
"yes, this is my idea!"
And just around the corner
someone else held the same thought.
We think
we are the only one feeling sad or irritated
and wonder what is wrong in our life,
why we feel this way...
and sometimes wonder is good.
But just around the corner
somebody else is feeling the same way.
Knowing that we are part of a
larger current
that carries all of "that" within,
helps
not to take it so personally...
the great and
the worst!

New

A new way of being is unfolding,
a knowing without the mind,
it requires a beingness on a deep level of trusting.
Not the intellectual knowing
is guiding the experience but
the radiating vibration of inner knowing
that is informed by the moment.

.

This asks for great boldness:
no more wrapping things up.
The truth has become so visible,
and the stepping away from one's truth has become so, so
uncomfortable
the invisible is so visible
and hiding oneself behind old ways or untruths has become so
painful
it leaves us with a
feeling of emptiness.
Yes,
it takes courage to step out
of the old patterns.
Heart is leading.

And where is the journey going?

I have no idea !
And that's a good thing.
It is a moment by moment unfolding
of our inner wisdom...
of the personal expression of your being,
of your heart.

Heart,

Energies are pouring into the heart
now
demanding more presence and realness,
alignment with your very specific gift,
your sound in the symphony of life.
If you feel so stuck in the old ways,
the old web of actions,
then what to do?

Anything,

with the intention of
freeing yourself.

And even so,

we are doing such powerful work with our hearts.
Be aware
of the necessity of balance in your being.
What I mean is
don't take on the role of the savior,
the giver only...
receive and allow being saved
just as much,
it will keep you humble
and inbalance.

Women

Women have two mouths!
Did you know that?
One above, and one below.
All women have the capacity to take in nourishment through
their upper and lower mouths,
just in different ways.
The lower mouth has the power to pull in the energy from the
earth.
The upper mouth eats from the earth.
The womb of a woman is connected to the cosmos, the void.
It is a place of great wisdom.
The lower mouth can speak of that wisdom.
The voice of the lower mouth is very precise,
straight forward,
true,
and knowing.

Receiving

True receiving is very profound.
It requires a letting go,
a surrender.
It is very essential to learn
the art of receiving
Many people get sick,
have accidents,
so they can finally let go
and receive into the depth of their being.
If you fight it,
it will trap you,
you will not grow.
The deepest healing
often happens in reverse.

N o w

The past, present, and future
are constructions of the mind.
The heart only wants to love in the moment.
If you can let go of your thinking of the past,
the future, and even of the present,

then you are here!

To move from the past into the heart, forgive.
To move from the future into the heart, trust.
To move from the present into your heart, breathe

E m b o d i m e n t

The greatest happiness,
lies in the moment.
We know that!
Not thinking about the future,
not thinking about the past,
just being with what is,
and expanding into it completely with every aspect of your being.
Embody the moment.
The moment becomes expressed through a body,
a being, and becomes real.

Then, we feel real.
So lets stop thinking
for a moment
and feel, taste, hear, see and touch
what is there right in front of us
with every aspect of our being...
no hesitation,
no holding back,
no fear,
just pure
curiosity.

Mystery

The invisible liquid connects us all.
Or is it air?
Or light?
Vibration?
Or all of it?
And so it is,
just like in the womb,
we are always in the liquid of
pure connection.
The only way to know for sure
is to open
the shell that contains you and allow
the wonder to unfold.
First there might be pain,
memories, or fears...
that's the shell's reason for being.
But once,
open
there is only love.

The Big Questions

...and then there is always the question
about purpose,
what am I doing with my life?
what is meaningful?
And I am wondering,
if I leave the question so big is it leading me well?
The bigness of the question pulls away my ground
And I start wondering if I am doing enough
Or counting what I have done.
I feel myself wanting to hold onto something.
Like Yes, I am doing this and that...
or the opposite, putting myself down
No, not really, I guess I am a looser!
Or
I don't know, I should know

I arrived at this:

i know it is not the accomplishments in my life,
whether or not I have built something that is visible
that makes me feel I have fulfilled my purpose.
I know it is how I live my life
that matters,
how I respond to the challenges and pleasures.
I know it is about finding my truth
and being willing to live it,
my courage,
my wisdom.
The moment I am responding with heart
in an impossibly hard situation
and I laugh—
because I know my heart is staying open
no matter what—
I feel I have arrived in my purpose.

T e n d e r

If you feel anxious and have trouble sleeping,
if the world's darkness is pushing on you
with its weight,
then take yourself by the hand
and smooth the inner worry with
your own heart,
stop your mind kindly
and whisper only goodness and kind words,
stroke your own skin and find solace
in the moment,
until you can remember the vast being
that you are,
eternal
and immense.

The Wisdom of
Not Knowing

Sometimes your life changes in an instant,
you fall off a ladder,
you get sick,
you loose someone you love,
or a veil is lifted from your life
and for the first time
you can see
the truth about something
you had wished was different.
The world you had built to make yourself comfortable
is disappearing
and you are feeling very uncomfortable
and full of so many new questions and feelings.
There is a faint feeling of gratitude
because you think it could have been worse...
and you have practiced to be grateful for your life.
But the thoughts and feeling are intense
and they are very difficult to contain,
they sometimes want to blame in anger

or collapse in sadness,
scream out in despair,
and then there is
love again.
An uncomfortable mix of feelings,
emotions, and questions....
You are in need of a sanctuary,
a place where you are held,
a kind and containing energy,
so you can find your breath again,
the one that guides you with wisdom
from this moment to the next,
in very small steps,
from moment to moment,
because it becomes clear that
you really don't know,
and that the wisdom of your journey
reveals itself in each moment
of not knowing.

Try that!

Sometimes life requires courage!
leap before looking
trust before knowing
love
just for the
sake of loving.

When Life Becomes Small

so you fall and hurt your back (or anything else)
and now you cannot move the way you are used to,
life and your body is demanding that you find another way,
demanding that you slow down.
you can be upset about it,
cry,
shout, and feel so angry
or beaten...
and, yes, all that sounds like a good plan,
but then,
be creative and find new ways to move,
to be,
to live.
it's a call for change and why wait,
and keep complaining with sorry feelings for yourself,
when there is a new way for you to explore,
turn around and look where the flow is
and, yes, the back (or whatever) will heal
because you are open again,
flowing with creative juices
that are healing.

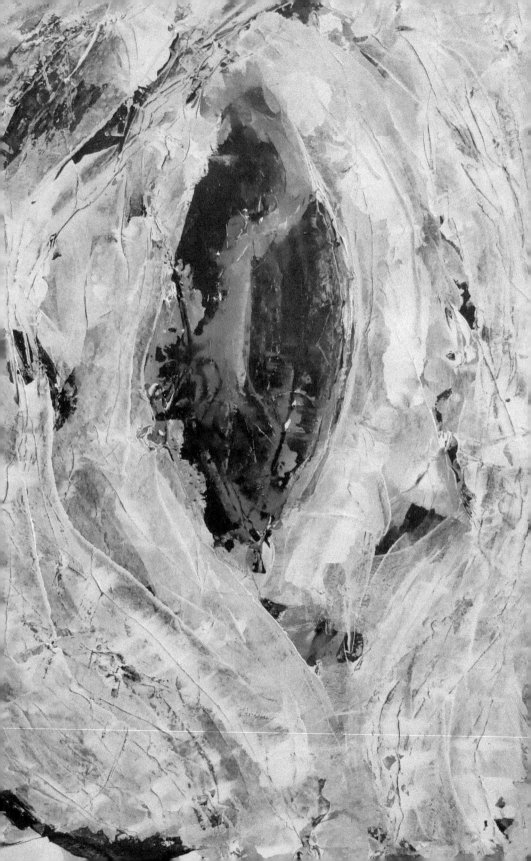

Self Love

Self love is a simple act of including yourself,
it is not something we do,
or all of a sudden remember.
It is more like an opening
to something that already is,
within us and around us.
When you start feeling from the center
of your being,
then you will know that love flows
through you,
like it does through all things.
It is the matrix that connects us all.
It is simple and most challenging
opening
because we don't believe
we are worth having that deep love
and connection to all things
and our life,
as we live it
has estranged
us.

Sehnsucht

Sehnsucht nach deiner Haut,
den weichen Lippen,
der Wärme deines Körpers
und sogar dem schwierigen Teil
deines Wesens,

Sehnsucht

In der Tiefe meiner Seele, suche ich
nach tiefem Erleben
Vielleicht ist es der Wunsch dich zu sehen,
der sich in eine Sucht verwandelt,
viellecht ist es eine Anfass-sucht,
Hör-sucht oder
Schmeck-sucht...
nicht nur Sehen-sucht

Meine Sinne suchen dich !

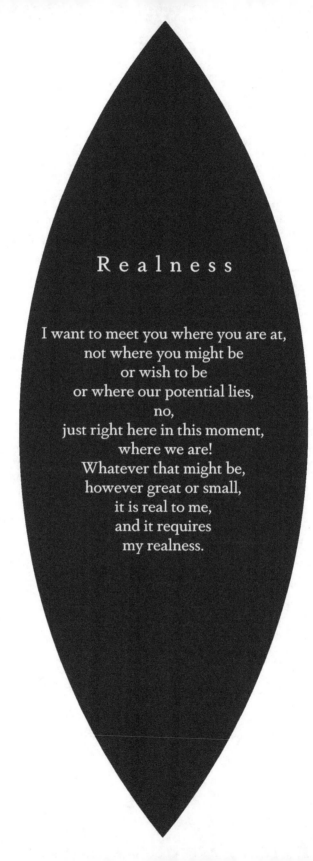

Realness

I want to meet you where you are at,
not where you might be
or wish to be
or where our potential lies,
no,
just right here in this moment,
where we are!
Whatever that might be,
however great or small,
it is real to me,
and it requires
my realness.

LOSS

When we loose someone
we love,
it hurts
We have merged with the other
in communion
and it is hard to let go.
Grieving is a powerful process of letting go,
and, yes, there is also the habit of having the
physical company
and love in one's life,
A gap opens,
a space that all of a sudden is un-occupied
and you find yourself still wanting to act
in the same way
as if nothing happened
and bump against the emptiness.
If you feel full
then the emptiness will feel rich
and when you feel empty yourself,
then it feels lonely.
But remember the gap is precious,
the emptiness rich,
and new life will come.
Just sit with me in the dark
gap of what is
and love will flow again.

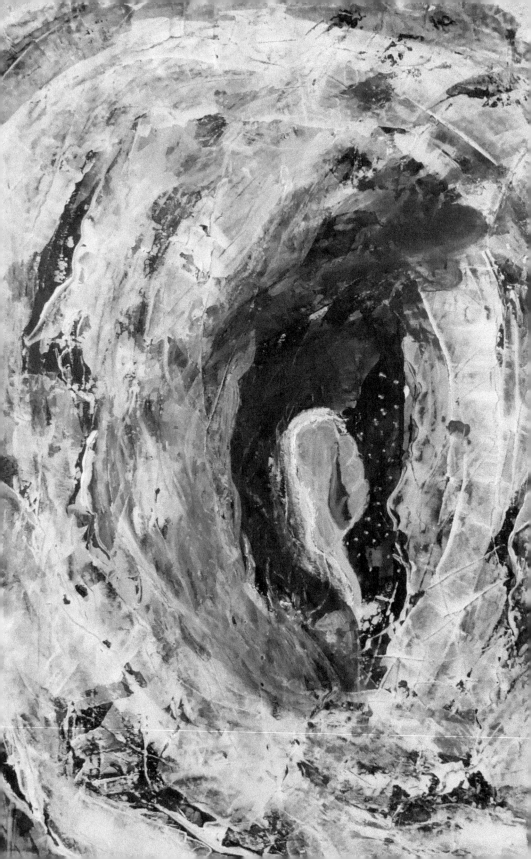

Pond

Today I looked at you over and over again,
your soft ripples
and deep currents move me,
even the trees cannot help but cast their image onto you
and you sway them carefully on your surface.
Every so often one of the little insects swim across your skin
and pull along with them ridges of your flesh,
others rest on top or drink of you, thirsty.
Me?
you hold in loving ways
and wash me clean of my sorrow,
so I am left with
happiness.

Vulnerable

Real vulnerability is a very humbling experience,
it is a matter of surrender,
of moving through our fears,
it is a very powerful state
and it is so attractive—
it literally attracts everything
we could want and more...
The problem is we have to own it,
be it,
become it.

No Worries !

One of the greatest gift
you can give to somebody you care about
is not to worry about them.
Work out your fear with yourself
and give them your trust
and love that they will be well
whatever happens.

Let's just let it all go,

all the ideas that you have about yourself,
all the expectations,
dreams,
all that you think needs to be different,
all that you think needs to happen...
no more holding up of some kind of a person you want to be,
no more pretending to be another.
Just let it go.
and
start loving now.

It is a practice:
loving what is,
loving as you are,
loving your life,
just loving for the sake of loving,
not because there is another,
not because of others,
but because you can.
And guess what ?
You will receive all this love from your own heart,
before it goes out into the world
It will change you naturally,
and will open so many places of love within you,
and you are ready to become,
to become you,
and when you are you,
you are everything,
You are connected to the field of love
that lives in everything.

To Let Go
and Listen

Most of the time,
when we hit a wall in our life,
we think it's because of others
and feel powerless or angry,
frustrated and defeated.
Even when we don't know what it is,
where it is, and how to shift it.
Know,
the key lies within reach of our
own inner world.
Once you shift inside
and let go of the blame
and hurt
there is a space
that opens within your being,
that space will teach you
how to heal and shift,
but first you have to let go
and listen.

Take Care of Yourself

Think of it this way...
when you are in an airplane
and there is an emergency the masks drop off the ceiling,
what are you supposed to do?
Put the mask on yourself first,
then on your child!
Otherwise you suffocate.
It is the same thing with love.
If you don't take it in first,
you will starve.

Empty

Let's leave the cup empty for a while
to see who or what pours in,
who comes to visit,
an unknown friend?
an unknown adventure?

I am ready for you.

Let me know life more deeply!
Let me not fear
what I do not know!
Let me open my being
so I am the spirit that flows in all,
so I am source itself,
so I am innocent
and pure.

Balance

One of the secrets to a balanced life is to know what our inner
state is.
Are we too full,
are we too empty?
Once we know where we are at
We can find out how to empty our inner fullness,
and how to fill our inner emptiness.
By becoming aware of our inner landscape,
a door to balance opens,
and we realize that may be we have projected fault onto others.
By being responsible for our inner world,
and what we need,
we gain power

The Power of
the Void

Just breathe,
sit in the dark
and breath in,
the creative flow
that is within
the darkness of not knowing,
breathe
it all in
as an ally
to create
to be
to trust
your own force

Love

It is simple...
you either trust in love, or not.
If you do,
she will envelop you entirely
and then who will you be?

love

C r u e l t y

it is very difficult to bear the cruelty of the world.
it is a practice to come out of denial of how cruel we are with
other human beings and especially with animals,
and the earth.
it is important to allow the sadness of that to enter into your being
so you can help transform the cruelty within yourself.
for that
you have to face your own life.
how am I contributing to cruelty?
how am I contributing to the transformation of cruelty into love?
do I take time to love the animals and plants,
the water
the sky
the trees?
have I even looked at them today?
am I eating meat that comes from a pool of cruelty?
am I taking more than I need?
am I taking responsibility for my energy and my being?
am I grateful for all that is given to me?
the sun the breath the wind the food... ?
ask the questions
and you will get an answer
in how to align more with the web of love that surrounds us,
you will feel more at home.
The more of us,
entering into the web of love,
the more the planet heals
and so do we.

Content

It is not so much what we do
that matters,
what is really felt by the whole of existence is
the energy we do it with.
We know that!
Why is it so hard to remember?

My mind wants me to be great,
have many projects,
be busy,
be famous,
talk about my accomplishments
so others admire me.
And, yes, for a moment,
I feel great
but it fades very quickly

Now

I've lost interest in accomplishing and producing,
my mind is scrambling,
what to say when people ask?

It is humbling to become,
to just be in the moment,
to do everything with a deep love for things and people.
The stories fall away, the achievements move inside.

You start looking very ordinary.

You better be ready for it!

Remember

It is always good
to be reminded,
that energy follows our attention,
our attention energizes.
Our intention is guiding the outcome.
The thoughts and feelings
energized with our breath
will grow.
We have immense power,
just by bringing consciousness to our breath,
we can move into the moment.
Then, with intention and attention, direct the energy.
Our heart knows,
trust that knowing.
It is a very powerful act of creation,
of being creative.

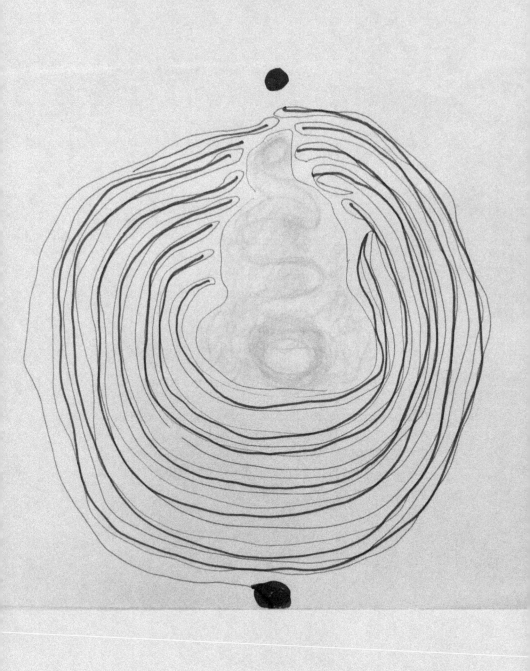

Is that you on the cross ?
(I am in a monastery, looking at a crucified Jesus)

Just like the ice on the river, I floated along,
still in the middle and faster around the edges
I floated well!
And then I realized
that where I really wanted to go
was under the surface.
Push me down,
I cry out...
but nothing happens.
Only the slightest tug on my heart reminding me to let go.
Let go of what?
where the last words of my mind
Sighs of oh's and ah's took over
and my inner parts started to melt.
Then my body stretched out like a cross,
heart in the center,
melting life into the forgotten places,
melting into the larger waters of love.
Like ice on the river, slowly.
And like he did on the cross next to me,
(dying into a new life)
This is not a one time deal,
this is an ongoing process
of staying alive, of becoming.
Of becoming present to what is below the surface
of who I am.
Shedding my skin over and over again on the cross like a snake.
Too bad we have forgotten our own skin-making
and just remember his suffering,
(he is still on the cross)
iI almost made us sinners forever.
But now I am resting in the hand that holds us all,

for a moment,
feeling grateful for the blood pumping through my veins,
the fire in my heart, the water of my ocean.
I am grateful for my presence and
equally for yours.

is it green or is it yellow?,
is it fight or is it surrender?
is it flow or is it contained?
is it fire or is it water?
is it all of it at the same time?

no matter what it is,
what's most important is
that you find your form,
your shape,
your energy,
so that your wisdom,
your vibration,
your heart comes forth.

we need it!

imaging that everything around you,
wants you to be that,
everything around you will rejoice,
and the ones that don't,
resist their
own awakening.

Intimacy

I will keep you on my skin, water,
and take you deep into my well,
you fall on me,
you surround me ,
you flow in my veins.
I have you on my tongue and in my belly.

Where are you not?

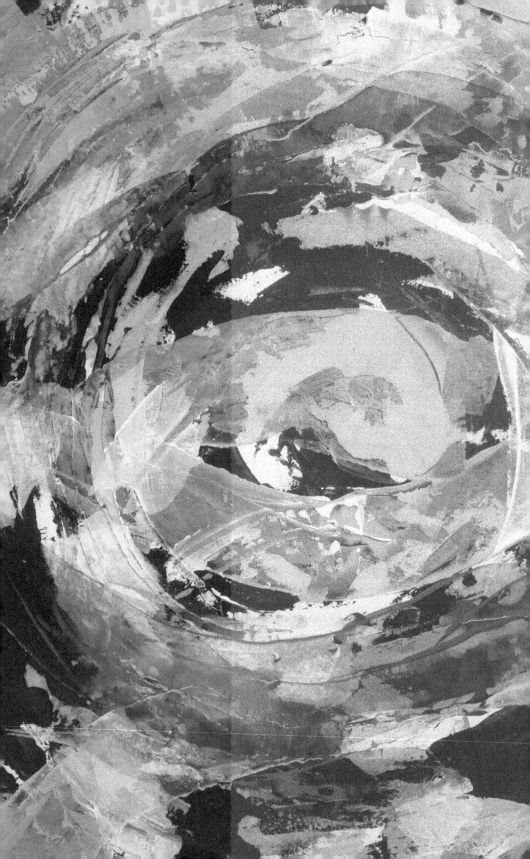

In-between

In-between

What to do when there is so much change?
So much is falling away and you don't know yet
What the new will be.
Who am I?
A voice questions within your being.
And what the hell am I doing here?
And it makes you nervous and anxious
because there is no immediate answer.
You are in the in-between!
A place of great power,
hard to bear!
It challenges all your thinking,
It challenges all that you feel is not ok within you.
It brings it to the surface.
In-between is a potent place,
it is the unformed magic
of what you are capable of creating in your life.
Nothing to do,
nothing to hold onto.
You can only enter by leaving all behind
and you can only handle it
by loving yourself,
Love will be your protection,
healing, and will
ensure you are creating exactly what you need.
So pet yourself,
tell yourself you are beautiful,
hold your heart and your belly,
talk in a soft loving way
so the small part within your being
hears you and starts trusting you.
Call to all your friends, in body and not,
to help you create this new phase in your life.

And TRUST
that you are in the making,
and all will be fine.
Even better, you are becoming who you are
without your mind knowing.

Fear is part of change

Fear is a sign that we are under pressure to change.
If the energy of fear gets big enough,
we open to change
we become willing to ask for help
we realize something is not right

if you want to grow,
fear says
grow now!
It is not about getting rid of fear
but use it's signal to grow,
it is about knowing
that something is challenging,
something is calling
to become
more

Relax

If you only can see one option,
you know you are stuck.
That knowing can soften your heart,
and relax your mind,
Now you know where you are,
how small the space is that your are in.
Your vision can widen,
your perspective change,
then everything in you
will relax.

Honest

If we have the courage to be very vulnerable about our fears,
our shame and judgments and we share openly
without blame,
it is a powerful way to deepen into your being.
We learn about our inner pain, insecurities,
and limitations.
We might find inside of us
that we have very strong ideas of how love should look like
and what we need to feel secure.

What we know for sure
is that it is a process
that can open new areas in the heart,
our old pains get a chance to become conscious,
and are allowed to just be.
We can not avoid the process
pretend we are there already,
that would be a great loss of an adventure
that has the potential to make
us whole.

Void
Creation

If you have the ability to sit
in the dark
of the un-manifest pool of the void,
still and present,
even just for a moment,
your presence will bring forth your song.
Your song will be brought into
the physical.
It is like imprinting your music,
your being, into the void.
The void will respond by manifesting
your imprint,
and so your song moves out of
the darkness into the light,
and more of you
is born.

Presence

if we can stay present to what is unfolding
with interest and curiosity,
even though we are not liking
what is,
we find out what it is really about
and there is a feeling of relief
when it finds its place
in the larger picture of life
and so
do we.

Sun

I am laying in bed,
sun licking at me though all the moving leaves.
Yes tell me,
I am listening to your wisdom
and enjoy your play on my skin.
The rhythm of the wind,
the shadows moving,
stripes of light
here and there.
Lets stay a little longer...
can I?
Thank you for waking me,
thank you for reaching between light and shadow,
trees and leaves.

Flying Fire

Tonight I stepped into the dark night,
naked
I left the day behind and moved
without fabric skin
into the dark presence,
as is.
I am here ! I have come ! I shout
Where are you,
all you magical creatures...?
Where are you, wind of spirit and
waving trees...?
I am here
Naked with my heart of pure love!
And slowly they show up all
around me,
they have been dancing all
night long
with their shining light.
Flying with fire.

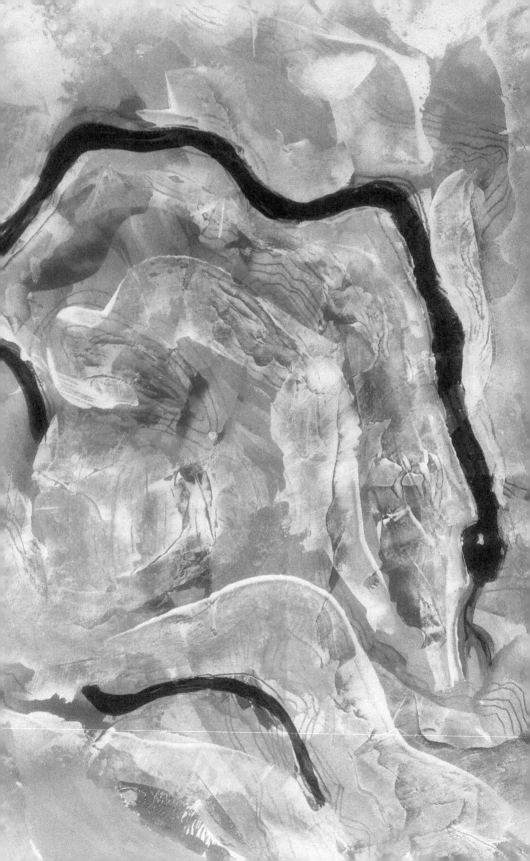

Spirals

If everything meaningful moves in cycles
and repeats itself over and over again with a slight twist,
and comes around again,
then why think in straight lines?
Think in curves.
There is no place to arrive at,
there are only places
to explore.

Beauty

I look at the immense beauty of nature
just outside my window
I feel in awe of creation,
I am thinking to myself,
I am so glad and lucky
that I found a way in,
as part of it all.
beauty has finally found a way in
and through me.

Stop!

I look around me
and wonder why we are so unwilling to be without
the usual same old,
same old,
always we seem to want to choose the same way,
we know it already!
why not choose a new experience,
so much time we spend on thinking, is this right or that right,
what is the right choice for my life...?

maybe all choices are right for our life,
you choose whatever
and then you experience,
and then you know.
That is how we arrive at knowing,
not by thinking and thinking and thinking and never arriving.
It takes courage to just dive into any experience,
it takes trust in yourself
that you can handle it
or trust that you will be fine
with whatever comes your way.
That kind of radical openess,

radical okayness is freedom.

You might be scared but you still go for it,
you are curious,
you are alive.
It is possible to cultivate a kind of a juice
inside your veins that makes you resilient and fearless,
it's called love for the self,
because you know when you feel love, or better yet,
are in the state of love,
you are full of it.

Too Much

I feel so full today,
full of things and thoughts and feelings
and I don't even know it...
just a slight feeling of crap,
of junk in the stomach and an occasional,
"I hate that" feeling.

too much!

I am irritated,
I am too full,
everything is tugging at me
and I am afraid I am going to explode
if I don't let go,

but how to empty?
how to move from the too-much-ness into balance,
into calm, friendly?

I close my eyes and say to myself...
no place to go,
no one to be,
nothing to do,
only blackness,
empty blackness
I am, I am, I am,
and for a moment with great discomfort of thoughts pulling
and feelings insisting

a tear runs down my cheek
oh thank you,
I am letting go
I sit in the dark and I am with it all
without anything,
nowhere
and
nothing...
and finally emerge out of the black liquid
with grace, balance,
space and deep gratitude.

W h y ?

I am wondering why
I have this nagging feeling today?
It is annoying me,
it follows me here and there.
I go left,
it goes left.
I go right, it goes right.
And then I realize and stop for a moment,
take a breath and turn towards it.
I feel a wave through me
and it leaves,
and I am at peace.
Everything needs attention,
loving attention

Really important

I am wondering what is REALLY IMPORTANT today?
Certainly not what is on my list,
what I think I have to accomplish.
Maybe taking a moment
and just making space for an answer without answering,
a listening into nothingness...
that space is
precious

What is

i am watching the rain fall on the grass,
on the leaves of the plants
and where it hits pools of water on the wooden deck,
it makes a circle,
quick,
and then gone,
a coming and going of circles
falling from above,
drops
and drops...
It is like a beautiful symphony of sounds and shapes.
It is refreshing
grateful for what is.

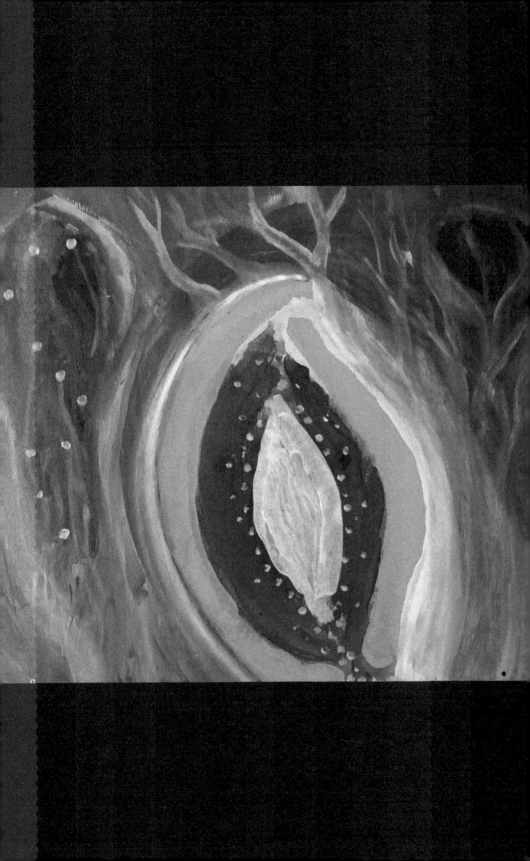

Truth

if something
is really meant to be,
there is no need to force anything.
if you try and force it,
then it becomes clear
that you have no trust
and are afraid that something
you have projected onto the situation becomes true
that has the potential to cause you pain.
it might be of great benefit
to investigate the projection
and work it out with a willingness to feel the pain.
then you might find yourself more free
to just be with the world
in a more
relaxed
way.

Beauty Within

Creating beauty
is an amazing practice of participation
in the creative flow of life.
It is your mirror.

How do I live the life
I am "meant" to live?

if something
is the question of the day
and so I start pondering.
My mind has many ideas of what
I need to do and accomplish
to feel good about myself,
how to leave a mark,
comparing myself to others
and look at my shortcomings...

it left me feeling crummy
and I thought to myself, why?
where is the love in this?

and then I realize
its just a game of my mind
and that my heart is only interested in being open,
feeling what's here in the moment,
and spreading love to myself and the air around me.
it is that simple...
a gesture of bringing or activating love inside myself.
then I start vibrating a wholly other song
that everything around me seams to respond to
and all of a sudden
I feel just fine
living my life as it is.
The meaning is in the opening
of my own energy.

S a m e   O l d

I look around me
and wonder why we are so unwilling to be without
the usual same old,
same old,
always we seam seem to want to choose the same way,
we know it already!
and why not choose a new experience,
so much time
we spend on thinking is this right or that right,
what is the right choice for my life...
may be all choices are right for our life,
you choose whatever and then you experience
and then you know,
that is how we get to know,
not think and thinking and thinking and never knowing.
It takes courage
to just dive into any experience,
it takes trust
into yourself that you can handle it
or trust that you will be fine with whatever comes your way.
That kind of radical openess,
radical okayness
is freedom.
You might be scared but you still go for it,
you are curious,
you are alive.
It is possible to cultivate a kind of a juice
inside your veins that makes you resilient and fearless,
its called love for the self,
because you know when you feel love
or better,
are in the state of love you are
full of it.

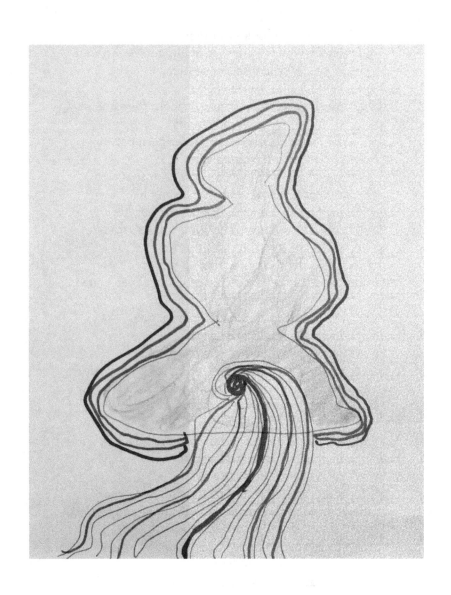

Small

The more
you constrict
your experiences
the smaller
you stay,
and in any case
there is no real safety,
just unlived
experiences.

Empathy

Very emphatic people
often have a great desire to help.
If we feel this way we have to make sure
we are always included in our giving,
that, at the core of our being,
we don't merge with the suffering around us,
which means we hold
the balance between beauty and pain.
They are always present,
together.
In the greatest pain and misery,
there is also the greatest beauty present.
If we can hold that awareness,
then suffering eases.
If we find ourselves so eager to help others,
it makes sense to invest some time
in the capacity to bear the suffering
before needing to fix it.

Holy

Whatever it is that makes us larger,
opens us more
to our true nature,
to our wisdom
and deeper love,
is something so precious and holy in itself.
It will slowly mend our holes of sadness,
aloneness
and despair
and make us
whole.

Vibration

Everything
in the universe responds to vibration,
you can tell when you talk to an animal or plant,
they respond to what you vibrate in your being,
not so much to what you say.
That is why it is important
you know what you vibe out.
We are so busy covering up our true inner state,
we are so afraid

and yet it is our vibration
creating the conversation,
not our words.

Everything

around us is
alive,
why are we not
treat it
that way?

Potential

Everyday has the potential to be a day of miracles.
Something that is beyond your expectation or imagination
can show itself,

and then what?

it is most likely
that that happens all the time...
but are we present?

Purpose

Everybody wants to know,
at some point in their life,
what their purpose is.
We all of a sudden,
feel empty without one,
we long for one,
we need one,
we do all sorts of things
to get one,
as if we are not enough
as we are,
and what we do or not do.
This moment of great unhappiness
is always
a call
to bring more love and wakefulness
into our life.
And then
maybe,
just being here as a loving,
awake being is plenty,
enjoying the experiences
as they come.

Learn

Every situation is an opportunity to learn and open,
to stretch to a larger wisdom,
to love
and be more present.
Don't go on automatic and
miss out.
Start asking questions
without answering them.
Start create space
to become you.

Drink

Whenever you drink water,
you are taking in everything
stored in the water since it has travelled
far and wide.
It is super intimate.
You take in the whole world...
everything that happened, good and bad.
We are exchanging with each other on such profound levels
all the time
and are often so unaware,
so asleep about it.

Pain

Don't be stingy with your love,
especially when it hurts.
The hurt is within your own heart
and it is the sign of opening.
Expansion of the heart can hurt,
it is like a frozen cold hand coming back to life,
it hurts.
The capacity to endure the pain of awakening is essential,
otherwise you will always shy away.
The capacity to know this awakening pain as good pain
instead of old abusive pain comes from trying it out,
comes from experience.
We often put ourselves in painful situations over and over again
to finally learn how to heal.
Stay conscious of the process,
stay awake through the pain,
once the emotional content empties,
there is very little pain left.
Then you are in the new expanse of
your love.

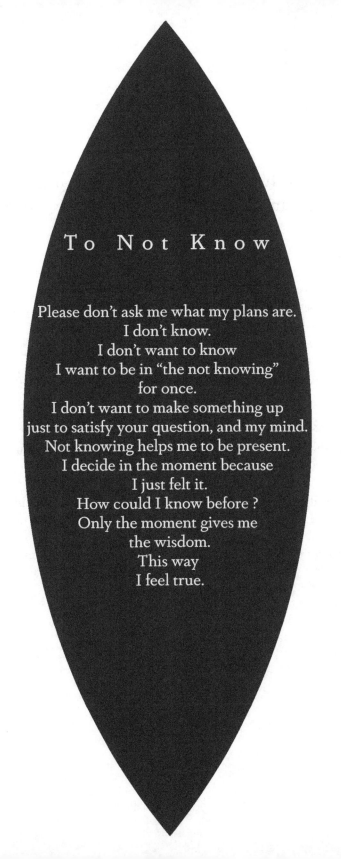

To Not Know

Please don't ask me what my plans are.
I don't know.
I don't want to know
I want to be in "the not knowing"
for once.
I don't want to make something up
just to satisfy your question, and my mind.
Not knowing helps me to be present.
I decide in the moment because
I just felt it.
How could I know before ?
Only the moment gives me
the wisdom.
This way
I feel true.

The deep longing
that makes you love more

I feel longing in this place and all around me
and it is tugging at my heart like soft yet insistent string pulling.
It says, "open up and embrace me like you have never done
before,
an embrace with everything,
as if this is the last and ever moment of your life!
"Open and let me flow inside you to tell you that I am in love
with you too." And so I ask,
Who are you?
You who tugs at my heart and I feel so deeply for?
You that has been here forever with your kind and warm eyes?
I wonder and
love you even more for you are mystery to me.
I am sitting here in the rain, drop by drop lightly touching my
skin, and the tree with its waving arms stretching around me.
How much I long for you .
And yet each time you touch me, I melt and grip and melt and
pray to let go
of what makes me love less.
For I want to love with a passion
Fire burning
flame

Do you want to play in the mud?

you ask,
and I say,
yes!

How did you know that in my deepest place,
I have been dreaming of slithering
and sliding like a snake,
soft belly against the slippery surface,
smooth skin to skin sliding,
disappearing
in the landscape like two silent creatures,
so very slow and alive,
disappearing
into animal skin
of mud.

Loslassen

Die schwarze Flüssigkeit lässt nichts von mir übrig,
Nichts !
Sie breitet sich langsam aus in meinem Körper
und verzehrt mich in ihrem unendlichen Hunger.
Mein Fleisch löst sich von meinen Knochen.
Meine Knochen werden weich,
Ich zaudere,
in tiefem Schrecken, Angst all das zu verlieren,
was mir lieb ist.
Angst der Welt zu entgleiten ins unbekannte Schwarze,
gesehnt und gefürchtet.
Gebe ich mich hin, wie ein Liebender der Liebkosung
und lass mich wegtragen von der langsam mich umgebenden
Dunkelheit,
des unbekannten Schwarzen
Oder halte ich,
mit fest geklammerten Fingern,
an den Kammern meines Herzens fest?
Sehnsucht,
löst den harten Griff meiner Finger und so tauche ich ein.
sanft und weich wie gestreichelt
auf einer nicht existierenden Haut.

Depression

And you might say
I don't know what connects me to my spirit,
I am so far away
and lived this life so long
that I have forgotten,
I am lost and there is no hope for me,
I am just a failure
and I feel sorry for myself,
I wish it were different,
I don't want to be here.
if we choose to live someone else's life,
it will make us feel like a failure,
how can one succeed in trying to live another's life!
all events will fail to encourage us to choose something else,
people that are very talented have a disadvantage,
because they will be able to be successful
in a life that is not necessarily their own.
Choose what gives you energy,
choose what makes you feel light,
be with people that you feel kindred with,
don't follow advice from others,
wait and start making a temple inside
where you can hear the small voice of your spirit,
if you don't hear anything at the beginning then have faith.
don't allow the old negative dark cloud to pull you back,
there is a light inside your being
follow it.

Clinging

Clinging to a love that imprisons
brings more and more suffering...
let go
and feel your inner turmoil,
its only inside your own inner walls,
there, you can free yourself,
the world will stay the same,
but you have the potential
to emerge free.

The spiritual Can-Opener

When you are so lucky
that you meet someone that opens you,
a presence that changes your life
for the better,
don't kill her or him
just because you cannot handle it.
You find yourself changed
and do not know what is up
or down in your world anymore
and want the presence that changed
you so deeply
to be there for you all the time.
Don't expect that,
they already did
what they where meant to do.
It is your turn to learn to handle the
new territory
and make sure the food in your newly
opened can does not spoil,
you need to eat it,
you need to know it.
Then the doors open to
immense gratitude
and a blessed life,
because that is how
you get to know yourself.
It is not them,
it is you,
they where just
the can-opener,
the food is
yours.

Beauty

I am looking at the beauty of a flower just next to me.
I am admiring her with great gratitude,
the flower's beauty,
in that moment.
I am thinking,
oh, I wish I where a bee
and I could dive into this beauty
and drink the nectar!
oh well.
i am just going to have to find 'my way'
my shape,
my being, and drink,
drink, and drink....
the nectar of beauty

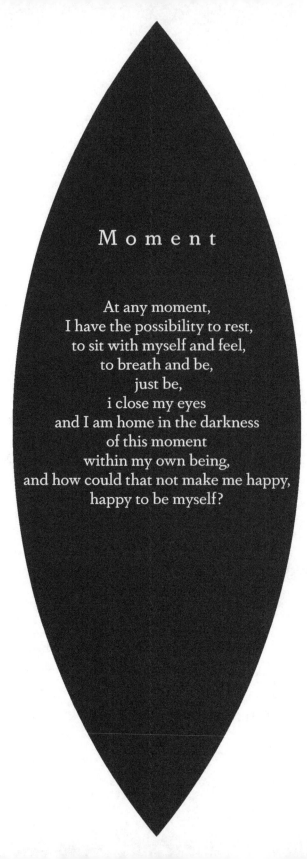

M o m e n t

At any moment,
I have the possibility to rest,
to sit with myself and feel,
to breath and be,
just be,
i close my eyes
and I am home in the darkness
of this moment
within my own being,
and how could that not make me happy,
happy to be myself?

Protection

It is our nature to assess things around us,
to check and figure out what is going on
so we can decide if we like it, how to respond,
safe or not...
and we do it fast without even noticing.
All our past experiences are helping to make that assessment,
which means it is a very personal choice,
individual, according to our past and inner beliefs.
In the moment we do that,
everything around us does that too,
and so the moment shapes an experience
that reflects all of our believing...
The imprint of bad experience onto a moment,
a person, an environment, leaves a sour taste for all involved
Then we think "oh, not again,
why are people so negative."
Or "ahh again ,
I knew it."
Or if it was a good experience.
"oh, I love you"

If this assessment has become rigid,
it is called judgment, when negative
and projection when it is positive.
If it is fluid and changes,
it is called checking out the situation.
If it is light and funny it is called
PLAY.

However it moves,
the key is inside and the tone of it,
is your choice.

Relations

Any good relationship
starts with the willingness and ability to listen and observe
mindfully,
to leave space
and attention for something to emerge from the other or oneself
and be noticed.
The interest and curiosity to learn something new about the other
and to meet the moment with a freshness,
or even innocence, brings tremendous gratitude
and love into ones life.
Because eventually it will reflect back
that all things are connected
in that space
of listening presence.

L o v e

...and what if you wake up in the morning
and you just really don't like yourself?
even the thought of feeling that,
makes you cringe.
and then you desperately search for somebody to love you,
to prove you wrong.
how come there is so little love inside?
why was it not planted like a beautiful seed
and how can you think
it's outside
and keep relentlessly trying to get it from someone.

just start planting inside,
you have the seed,
it's in your own belly,
it's in your own heart,
it's everywhere inside you,
you just have not looked.
and all existence will love you back,
the trees,
the water,
the sun,
the wind with the soft touch,
the animals and
also the humans
but love will be different then
and your heart will be light.

Destiny

All colors and shapes of pollen fly
through the air
to find a plant far away,
carried by the wind as its ally,
it is meant to make love to
bring forth another flowering,
a fruit.
Some of the pollen has
small Velcro like spots
that attach to something or someone
to be carried away to another plant of the
same species, and does it know,
if it will ever arrive?
Everything around us
Trusts in an adventure,
in an unfolding
and does its part no matter
what the outcome might be.
I think it is the same
for us, it is in the doing
of our part, in our attempt
to full fill our destiny,
not in the end result,
There is no failure,
there is only becoming
present.

Teacher

if there is struggle,
then it is time to invent something new,
take advantage of the call to change,
to open to something different,
so that a new flow can refresh
and nourish your life.

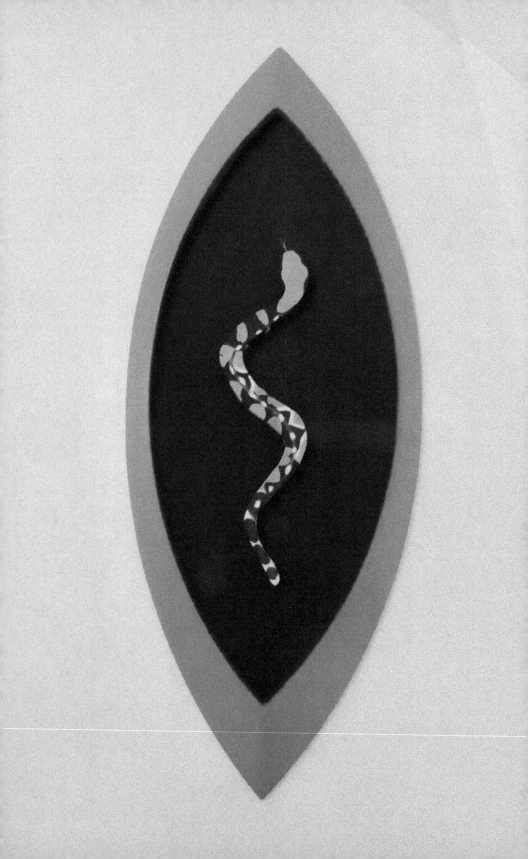

Serpent

All my life you have been with me,
in my dreams,
over and over again,
in my path,
stopping me in my tracks,
stretching out of the grass up in the air
with elegance,
focused power,
demanding my presence and realness.
I know you bring me wisdom
a powerful energy of awakening.
I can feel it,
scary and real,
graceful and swift.
Nothing in me can resist you,
and so I follow you into the
Mystery.

Mistakes are Ideas
of the Mind

You expected,
planned, and agreed
but then it happened differently.
Sometimes mistakes serve more that you can imagine.
They can be a form of guidance.
Mistakes can create openings,
allow new discoveries.
They bring more information,
more experience.
"Trust what is...,"
the voice says inside of me,
after I just made a terrible mistake
"...and stay alert for how it plays out
and what it brings forth in you or others."
It is needed.

And so,
I serve by not feeling bad about myself
and stay present.

Becoming

Sometimes
I hear the kindest and loving voice inside of me,
so soft and thoughtful,
so heartfelt
when this voice speaks,
I feel so endlessly moved
– it makes me cry,
and in that moment
I become more like the voice.

Wake Up !

We need challenges!
otherwise
we fall asleep even more,
they push us into new territory,
otherwise our lives stay small,
once awake,
challenges don't exist anymore,
they blend into
the flow
of life.

Closed Door

"If one door closes, another is opening"...
is an old saying
it takes creativity to find the opening,
don't keep staring at the old closed door
and feel sad,
start moving in the dark,
even though you do not know,
trust your being
explore what else is there for you to find ?

A whole universe
to explore!

Love Making

When we make love,
I feel the cosmos,
the dark wide sky,
the planets,
light and dark swirling together,
seeds of light flowing,
I take them all in,
deep inside my body
and feel pregnant with mysterious light,
so far away and
yet, so close.

Creative Force

We all have an amazing creative potential,
it is our nature,
allow it to direct the flow of your life
and trust it.
The impulse does not come from the brain,
but from deep within,
where we know.
just jump in
and trust that you are able to handle it
if not,
then we learn,
there are no mistakes,
there is no failure,
only
ongoing experience.

Such longing
in us for that holy place

So we travel far to be reignited into our own inner wisdom,
thinking others have it to give.
And sometimes they do,
unexpected.
And often when we are most vulnerable
and deeply struggling,
it opens us to receive,
what already is.
Maybe the travel to a distant place,
worn us out,
maybe the kindred spirit that presented itself
maybe the terrible tragedy that occurred,
opened something
that we have kept closed for so long
and have been silently longing
and unconsciously protecting
with hope
for more life.

To Be Close

We all have such longings to be close to the natural world,
to the animals,
the plants and each other,
but we have numbed ourselves in order to live the way we do in
this civilization, our life .
We are killing and mistreating people,
plants and animals every second,
without respect for life,
there is no reverence for the source of life in all living beings.
So far removed,
we are,
from being in right relationship with the natural world and each
other.

So far removed from ourselves.

So lonely, so separate, feeling so numb with no awareness.
There is a need for change,
a need to wake up,
to un-frost the numbness,
to be able to be closer to oneself,
to allow the grief of what happened melt the icy heart.
It's not easy to see how it really is and to be willing to change
your inner landscape to a way of love.
A kindness unfolding within
starts
in the heart.
Unthawing....
And to consciously bear the unbelievable cruelty
that is such a natural part of our world,
is not a small task.
Lets start with being kind to ourselves,
May be this is the way to heal !
How it all comes together in the powerful vessel of the heart,
to balance.

Shift

The most important aspect of awakening
is to be able to shift your perspective,
to allow other perspectives
without feeling a loss or a threat.
if you ever feel like the world has
wronged you,
then shift into yourself as being the world,
make yourself larger,
because you are.

if you are really honest,
you are
the one creating

Good and Bad

Each persons perspective, their life,
gives a glimpse at existence itself.
It reflects a manifested Divine aspect of the Source,
that is why it is so precious and amazing to get to know people's
perspectives, because through the other person you get to
understand and expand your knowing of source,
of the Divine flow.
Good or bad, nice or yucky, it is still all a reflection of what we
call God.
So if one can travel between perspectives,
see and experience another without judging, fear or clinging...
then one gets to experience Divine source manifested.

Yes I think to myself that sounds true
but why include the "bad" stuff.
The things that have the potential of killing,
The unbearable cruelty ?

The darkness can create such inner pain and grief
it is hard to allow that.
and yet I know
it's true.
It all belongs.
and so
we do

The Seed of the Void

The great nothingness,
the blackness of unborn potential,
is the nature of what is to-become.
It is a place of rest,
before creation happens.
If you wish to carry more of this
powerful place within you,
this fertile ground,
and want to plant a seed in your body,
plant this one

To Become Real

The greatest gift
you can give yourself
is to deeply feel inside and take time to find out
what brings you joy,
what is true for you.
We forget!
We get swept away by the outer world
of how we need to be in order to function.
We think it's what we've learned,
what everybody likes,
but if you listen deeply
in the space of not knowing
and are willing to wait until your inner timid voice comes forth
and speaks
you are becoming yourself,
you are becoming real,
you are appearing,
then it's time to make
THAT happen,
no matter what.

The Right
Soil—
The Right
Moment

Everything in nature needs its perfect
environment to grow,
more or less.
When the seed decides to germinate,
the temperature is perfect,
the moisture is correct,
the nutrients are there,
to open and become.
Think of it the same way for yourself
and create the atmosphere
for your spouting, your flowering.
What it is that you need
to flourish?
Don't hold back and stay small.
Try,
and don't throw yourself back
into the same unprepared territory
that will not support you. To find what?
A deep desire to know who
you are, you say.
I understand,
but if the experience
repeats itself
and you find yourself
at the same spot, then let
that be a message
to be kinder.

So Unbearably Vulnerable

Deep within my heart
is an unbearably vulnerable being.
I try to hide her because she is so breakable.
She feels everything with such intensity.
She loves life
jet feels so sad at times.
She believes in love and does not understand
why this world is the way it is.
She swims in a field of energy that connects all.
The more she comes forward and becomes visible,
the deeper my experience of life is.
She pulls me deep under the surface.
And a breath could kill her.
She has deep presence and gratitude for life force
and many things that are normal in this world, are cruel to her.
She needs her own rhythm, her own timing, no pressure, no
pushing,
just allowing presence.
She loves to sing and dance with the wind,
naked

Practices:

*If you feel inspired by my poems then in this section of the book
you will find actual practices that help to bring forth awareness,
consciousness and an open energy system.
They are very practical and interesting, they come from
different traditions and some of them I came across in my own
experimenting,
they helped me!
Please enjoy this unusual collection of
explorations.*

Void
Meditation

emptying
close your eyes
sit in the darkness,
still
content,
nothing to do,
nowhere to go,
no one to be,
just be
in this moment
with your breath
and let it all empty,
don't hold on,
just this moment,
this darkness,
this breath,
just you
and the dark,
resting
in
nothingness.

Black mirror practice
to enter into the void
communicate with spirit
travel to far places
plant a seed of the void
inside you body

You will need a black mirror for this practice and a small bee wax
candle.
You can make a black mirror by painting the back of a framed
glass black, bless and add protection to the object.
The black mirror is a doorway, like any mirror is.
Bless it so it serves for your growth and leaning and brings forth
the best in you.
At any time in the night, you can enter into this special
mysterious encounter with the help of the mirror.
Set up your candle to the side of you,
so you can see a slight reflection of yourself and sit straight in
front of the mirror.

Start with saying a prayer for protection during your exploration
and surround yourself with beautiful energy in the space you
created with the prayer.
Sit still
slowing down everything inside you
your breath
your thinking,

allow the day to drop off you
allow shifting into
a magical space,
let your heart open and know that loving is your
greatest protection in any exploration and encounter.
If you are able to let go of your identity and melt into the vastness
then
your image in the mirror will disappear,
there will not be a reflection of you anymore.
your state of openness and dissolution of your persona
will be confirmed in the disappearing of your reflection.
This means you let go.
Letting go is not easy, sometimes it requires tears or other releases.
This in itself is an amazing practice
sit and let go till your reflection has disappeared!
sacred space opens
Once open and your reflection has disappeared
you are entering into the sacred space of the void,
you have left everything behind,
you are going
naked
The void has access to all.
You can ask questions,
you can travel
you can just sit in the vastness
and enjoy and marvel at existence itself

If you can bring back a seed of the void
plant it in your body
it will guide you in mysterious ways because it always keeps a
space open within you to know, to explore, to just be.
All magic comes
from that space.
Please close with a prayer and gratitude

The tool of the black mirror is from the path of pollen tradition.

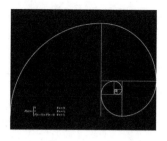

Practice to help with pain and emotional upset that manifested in your body

Start with saying a prayer to feel safe and surround yourself with
beautiful energy in the space you created.
Sit or lay down whatever is comfortable for you.
And start moving your body in very small movements, however
they occur without thinking, slowly, remember your animal body.
Breathe consciously while you are doing that,
Then start focusing on the area of discomfort and imaging a
beautiful energy or an amazing moment in your relationships
with a person or nature, make it nourishing soft and delicious,
start calling forth that energy,
soft kind, warm, cozy and if you can add a sexual note to it, it
will augment the healing energy, breath that energy into the
discomfort, try not to think
Just focus on breathing this delicious warm soothing arousing
energy.
you can also just start with soft warm and then add other
attributes.
Let it spread like a warm liquid.
Your mind will try and deter you and make you think of the pain,
emotional pain, the pain body as Eckhart Tolle calls is wants to be
fed, try not to feed it.
Stay with the jummy feeling and start making a sound of mhhhhh
With it or any other sounds that brings a feeling of enjoyment.
Inhale and on the out breathe add the mhhhh sound
And every so often just breath out with a ocean wave sound

breath, it a breath that uses the exhale against the throat, this will dissolve the boundaries and you will be able to take the other yummy energy in better.
If you need more grounding then start squatting
The body will respond to the goodness of this energy, it is vibrational medicine.
Please close with a prayer and gratitude

Practice to merge with your
surrounding and fill you with
energy. To feel energized,
supported and nourished
And may be even float !

We perceive ourselves as separate from the energy field around
the plants, animals, other people and the earth it self, but we are
not.
We all swim in a kind of a soup together pretending to be
separate,
It takes a lot of effort.
If you are willing to open and be held by the energy field around
you, you will be surprised how much you are receiving in terms
of nourishment, energy, support and love.
You will be able to move in ways that your muscles cannot
support, these movements don't make sense to our regular
movement patterns, we think its impossible, but the surrounding
energy makes it possible, it just not a visible energy to us.

Once you are one with the energy around you
you are feeling in love with what is.

Let's practice this with a small meditation.
Its good to start small to gain trust and then expand.
Say a prayer so you feel safe and protected in this space you are
creating.
Then close your eyes,

imagine that you are dissolving your boundaries,
Use an out breath that makes a sound like a wave, the air hitting
the back of your throat, it sounds like the ocean
and sink deep within, keep breathing this way till you feel clam
and diffuse,
it will help "you" to disappear.
Then imagine that under your chin is a very potent space, it is
alive with energy and it is expanding and ever so slowly it is
lifting your chin up, ever so slowly this outside potent space is
lifting your chin, no effort
you are so relaxed
and just here
The space around you is doing the work.
you are being moved so, so, slowly,
the slowness is important.
You are using your imagination to open the space around you,
you are imagining it being alive and that it is moving you without
effort.
Then once your chin is up, imaging the contrary now the space
is shrinking and ever so slowly takes your chin down, it takes
forever...
You stay relaxed, no work....
And if you keep practicing the expanding and collapsing of
energies around you with you staying relaxed you will discover
that there are other ways to move that with your muscles, very
relaxed and flowing, supported by the nothingness around you,
that is potent space.
You can apply this to many areas outside your body.
Use your imagination to help with this magic unfolding.
The more you trust the potent space the more you will feel the
nourishment and energy streaming inside.
This can allow you to generate endless energy.
May be this is how saints float.
They are carried by invisible lines of energy, invisible ether.
Once it become a reality that the space around you is alive
you will be able to move very differently, buoyant.
First use your imagination to get started and engaged with the
aliveness around you
It will develop into knowing
and trust.

Close with a
prayer and gratitude

This practice is from continuum movement
by Emily Conrad D'aoud.

Practice to be able to shift
perspective
Embodied Shape shifting

In many of my poems, I write about that
being able to shifting perspective is one of the greatest skills
that you can start to know source itself
by taking on many perspectives to one topic.
There is no absolute truth
just perspectives.
They are like flashlights shining from different angles on the same
object, all of them light up another aspect,
we need them all in order to get to know the object.
So to challenge yourself and what you believe,
you might want to try this!
Start with saying a prayer to feel safe and surround yourself with
beautiful energy
Pick a topic you fear or one you are curios about
or have a lot of judgments, like old people or ill people...
once you know what it is
I would like to invite you to become that, that person.
So get an outfit, a wig, a hat, a dress, a cane, a hump,
Whatever it is, dress yourself up as such.
Act like that person you despise, may be the homeless on the
street or the old person that is about to die, a blind person or the
sleazy salesperson or whatever it is for you, become that.
You can also start with something easy that you always wanted to
be,
for a day, for a few hours

Move out into the world as that other, and see what you learn,
about where you live within yourself.
Even just for an hour...
If you can light up another wildly different perspective
within your being that is a true gift,
It will open your heart even more

Before you start say a prayer to create a safe and beautiful space
for yourself
and close the space after you finish with a prayer and gratitude.

Titration between dark and light:
Practice to achieve oneness

(Titration is a process of adding base liquid in small amounts to a liquid of acid to determine concentration, since the liquids will change color when neutralized.)

A process to weave from your greatest pain
to your most pleasurable experience
in order to find balance and neutrality.
This is a healing way to join opposites.
The most amazing experience of love and connection
and the saddest, lonely and deep painful suffering moment
come from the same source, they are one.
When one is present the other is also present.
That is the meaning of the yin yang sign.

One of the practice, I want to teach, is how
to travel the full array of life's feelings,
from the most ecstatic to the most miserable
and to be able to stay present.
If that is mastered and one can feel all the facets of these
experiences
without interruption, from one end to the other,
the circle is closed
you have transcended,
which means pure presence.
Presence as a human,
present as a divine,

present as a spirit,
present in all ways
and always

If you wish and feel overwhelmed start small, as small as possible
with your pain and your happiness.
Start from where you can feel something, and then start widening,
deepening so that you always stay connected to yourself,
to your feeling realm.

Start with saying a prayer to feel safe and surround yourself with
beautiful energy in the space you created with the prayer.

Close your eyes
l like your to imaging your worse painful incident in your life,
nightmare, and I would like you to consciously allow that
experience to occupy your energy, your energetic body
if you don't feel comfortable with allowing this feeling to be all
over you body, just confine it somewhere where you will allow
this feeling to come forth.
So for a few minutes we are going will be there together.
Together but actually You are going to be by yourself, lonely and
separate because that is the nature of pain.
It is challenging to consciously call up this place with our bodies,
there are many defenses in place, just stay with it with your
intention of opening that difficult place and see what comes forth.
Once you are in it and feel your worst nightmare to whatever
degree
then I would like to invite you in the opposite direction, we
are now adding the other liquid to this experience, this is the
Titration.
Now start imagining the most ecstatic, beautiful experience
may be In nature, may be with a lover, the most loving, the most
connected feeling.
Whatever it is just bring that forth, everywhere in your body, in
every cell, if you don't feel comfortable bringing it forth in all of
your cells, only bring it forth in some of the cells whatever you
can consciously hold, one cell will work.
And lets stay there, for a few moments, feel that, as much as you
are able,

the most pleasurable, enjoyable moment.
Now we go back to the so very difficult to bare experiences that
have pained you,
stay for a few minutes
and we go back to the most pleasant and beautiful experiences in
your life and stay for a few minutes.
Does that feel familiar?
Life moves in waves
So we are moving back and forth, between the two states, from
the pain to the love and back to the unbearable to the joy and
each time we revisit we find there is a little bit of joy in your pain
and sadness in your ecstasy
And may be a feeling of depth opens.
It is like you have a light liquid and a dark liquid, every time you
move between the two, one liquid to the other, each time, you
take a little bit of one to the other until both of them have joined
and the color of your inner being changes.
And then lets see how that feels?
See what happens
What color you have become?
Please close with a prayer and gratitude

Walking meditation: Infinity Embodiment practice of working with opposing energies Sacred eight Meditation.

The symbol of the infinite 8 contains the opposite
You confine yourself to walking the figure 8,
like the bee does in her dance of communication,
Then you can weave together the opposites.
The symbol is powerful and you can bring it alive with your
energy.
One part of the 8 is the dark the other the light, one side is sad the
other is happy and in the middle you rest, the resting point, still
between the two, the knot
A special place of power
You can choose to move between many move opposites in your
walk
You will need 2 stones, smaller that your hand
but visible for you on the floor.
Start with saying a prayer to feel safe and surround yourself with
beautiful energy in the space you created.
Then take your two stones and move them from the center, knot
outward so they are in the center of each part of the 8, make it
a conscious act that with this gesture you are opening the space
between the know and the 2 sides.
This will orient you where to walk the stones mark the center of
each part of the eight.
Test it so you feel comfortable walking.

Hold your hands in a special position that reminds you that you
are walking in consciousness.
And decide what your topic is which of the opposite
you want to explore in your life.
And then you walk along the imaginary line of the eight around
your stones, walk and walk through the landscapes of your inner
worlds and stay awake
Between 2 poles and rest in the middle.
Explore, dance, move your energy...
About 18 min more or less
And then start closing the space by bringing the stones together in
the knot, the center
with gratitude,
close with a prayer
you can walk this shape for many reasons, it does not have to be
opposites.
This is a meditation from the path of pollen tradition

Woman Meditations

*(men also have a womb, it is energetic in nature, if you wish
as man you can also do these mediations with your energetic
womb.) imagine !*

first exploration:

*The Yoni meditation for feminine power and connection to the
earth
This mediation awakens the temple of the womb,
And impersonal sexual aspect of the yoni
Say a prayer to create a safe and beautiful space for yourself*

Please wear a skirt, no underwear
Sit or walk on the earth and start feeling the connection between
your yoni and the earth.
Squat every so often and focus, invite the energy flow between
your lower mouth and the earth.
Start the conversation
Listen to the exchange, open the door,
create a space within you where you can listen to the
conversation that is going on between your yoni and the earth.
Move and hold yourself in a place of curiosity.
We have lost that connection and rarely take time to listen.
Opening a space for you to listen to your yoni and womb is very
beautiful.
Even if you do not hear anything at the beginning,
the space matters.

If you hear a sound, a word, a something
start expressing it.
That will start the flow, however absurd it may sound to you,
go for it
Release the feelings that are keeping you from expressing.
If you stay in this process the conversation will become clear,
Even just the space that you are opening with your intension to
heal and listen is sacred and powerful in itself.
And know that with time you will start hearing a voice within
your womb, full of wisdom and clarity.

Then you know you have opened your lower mouth.
The womb and yoni has great wisdom, it has a voice just as your
upper mouth can speak, your lower mouth can also.
The voice of the lower mouth is oracular,
Full of wisdom.
Opening your lower mouth will create an energy flow between
earth and you, this is very healing, it gives you power, it will
nourish you deeply and you feel you have arrived home
It is also very healing for the earth.
Please close with a prayer and gratitude

This mediation come from the path of pollen tradition

second exploration:

Yoni meditation for feminine power and connection to the earth
This mediation awakens the temple of the womb,
And impersonal sexual aspect of the yoni

Begin by saying a prayer that you are safe and held in a pure
space, so you feel you can let go.

Sit comfortable with skirt, no underwear and
put your consciousness on your womb and yoni,
add your hands if that helps to focus
And start breathing.
Imagine taking the breath with your yoni,
Imagine there is a delicious energy that you can breath in with
your yoni.
Please add a sound to the out breath, a sound that reflects your
feelings.
Keep breathing in to your yoni and then with your sound release
the breath.
The sound, your sound will help to open the feelings that are
closing the energy flow.
Allow the feelings to flow...
The sounds are powerful, the sound of your own voice is a great
healer.
Please close with a prayer and gratitude

third exploration:

Yoni meditation for feminine power and connection to the earth
This mediation awakens the temple of the womb,
And impersonal sexual aspect of the yoni

Begin by saying a prayer that you are safe and held in a pure
space, so you feel, you can let go.
Then start with the position on all fours.
You imagine that behind you is the most beautiful energy....
And your yoni is reaching for it, with the in breathe you pull that
energy into your womb, the most sacred and beautiful energy is
now inside of you,
you are with your back bent down, in a cow position,
then you start moving this sacred energy up your spine and slowly
bent your body into cat position, back up to the sky, while you are
doing this, you breathe out your upper
mouth towards the earth.
Breathe in through your lower mouth your yoni, all this
nourishing sacred energy and breath it out your upper mouth
with a sound, your sound, while bending your back down and
then slowly up, like a cat.
Again breath in, on all fours with back curved down into the
womb and yoni and then slowly bend your back up and breathe it
out the upper mouth with your sound, then again....
Until your start feeling a connection between your lower mouth
and upper mouth
Even just being able to take in energy into your womb is a
beautiful practice.
Please close with a prayer and gratitude

fourth exploration:

Yoni meditation for feminine power and connection to the earth
This mediation awakens the temple of the womb,
And impersonal sexual aspect of the yoni

Say a prayer to create a safe and beautiful space for yourself
A woman can have access to the universe through her womb and
yoni, the void in the womb space is directly related to the void in
the cosmos.
Within the womb there is a gateway to the greater worlds.
It requires great letting go to be able to travel through this
opening.
Once you have opened the communication between lower mouth
and upper mouth and lower mouth and earth,
you can start exploring this gate within your body.
Your connection to the void,
the unborn potential,
the vast and never ending
of existence itself.
Please close with a prayer and
gratitude

Lower mouth meditation for woman or man with an imaginary womb to increase the lower mouth intake of energy into the body

Sit in a comfortable back straight way
and say a prayer to create a safe and beautiful space for yourself

Inhale and exhale consciously and prepare yourself, move your
energy inwards.
Close your eyes and feel the darkness, you just created all around
you.
Become still
Then inhale for a count of 6 seconds and hold the breath for
6 seconds, breathe out slowly in equal timing, while you are
breathing out, your are pulling the muscles tight in your sex
organs and rectum and pulling energy into your yoni and womb.
Hold for 6 seconds
All breaths and transitions are 6 sec. or at least equal in time.
So the in breath, hold, the out breath, hold are equal in time.

You pull in the energy into your yoni womb space with the out
breathe,
this creates a vacuum und energy is sucked in,
When you inhale earth energy is distributed in your body and
auric field.
It is very powerful to hold your breath, on full and on empty.

It resets your nervous system.
Breathe in this pattern for 6, 12, 18 min or as long as you wish
You are nourishing your body with earth energy or whichever
energy you decide to pull into your yoni and womb.
You are taking in nourishment through the lower mouth in form
of energy.
Close the space after you finish with a
prayer and gratitude
This mediation come from the path of pollen tradition

Mirror meditation to increase self love
Which is the foundation of all love.
The fertile ground for all other love to grow.

For this meditation you will need a regular hand mirror.
And enough light so you can see yourself clearly in the mirror.
Bless the mirror, since all mirrors are pathways, set up a positive
serving healing energy in the mirror.
Please say a prayer so you feel safe and protected in this space you
are creating as a preparation for this meditation.
Sit with your eyes closed and sink into a deep feeling of love, may
be a lover or a beautiful animal connection,
A place
A person you love
And then when you are full of that
Slowly and consciously look at your self in the mirror without
loosing that deep place of love,
Stay alert in your consciousness, if you all of a sudden start
thinking,
Avoiding...
just notice what your responds is.
Don't get into fixing things that you don't like in your face
Just be there looking with love.
Look into your own eyes with love.

See how long you can handle it.
Min 3 min.
And repeat for a month, a moon cycle, everyday to look at your
own eyes with love.
You might see your own soul looking back at you.
Close the space after you finish
with a prayer and gratitude

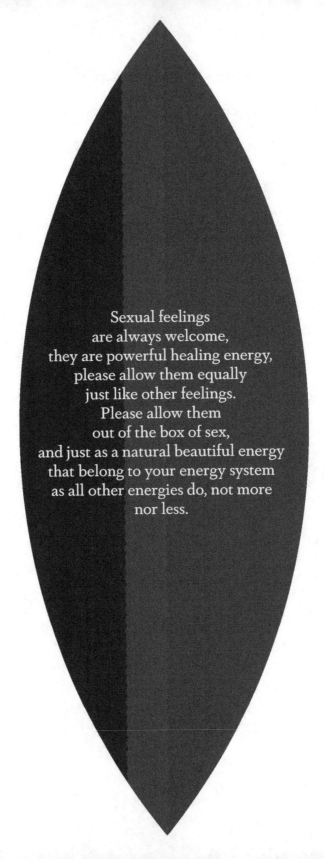

Sexual feelings
are always welcome,
they are powerful healing energy,
please allow them equally
just like other feelings.
Please allow them
out of the box of sex,
and just as a natural beautiful energy
that belong to your energy system
as all other energies do, not more
nor less.

Gratitude to the unseen world for their inspiration and support. My great desire to see what is not visible has inspired much of my art.
And to all my teachers big and small a big thank you.
Deep gratitude to Dror Ashuah for his continual support in publishing these poems, and for his love and presence in my life. I don't think this book would exist without his encouragement.

Deep thank you to Annette Knopp, Joseph Jastrab, Gail Staub and Alexandra Spadea for their friendship and words.

Gisela Stromeyer is an internationally well-known artist. She has been trained as a dancer, architect, healer, and teacher.

She completed and taught at Barbara Brennan School of Healing, completed the School of Enlightenment and Healing and the School of Intentional Living and studied Continuum Movement with Emily Conrad since 1995. She loves moving expression of her inner world and making the unseen world visible.

She is a Kundalini Yoga teacher and studied the power of sound with Don Campbell and many other sound healing methods. For the last 25 years she has explored different modalities of healing that include shiatsu, channeling, trance states, shamanism in the form of vision quests, the Bon Religion of Tibet, Singalese Shamans in Sri Lanka, the Shipibo Indians in Peru and the Path of Pollen, a Mystery School based in England. She is making her own herbal remedies and likes to communicate with the elements, animals and plants—and, yes, with humans too—to create a sacred and blessed world. Bees and horses keep her company.

Being creative in any way that life brings to her makes her happy. She is a mystic and an explorer, and her expeditions start inside her own inner world.

Only later in life did she become a poet.

Gisela is the director of Heartpulse Partnership, a non-profit organization bringing more heart into the world.

www.stromeyerhealing.com | www.stromeyerdesign.com
www.heartpulsepartnership.com